10 spiritual lessons
you can learn from
your dog

10 spiritual lessons you can learn from *your dog*

Joanna Sandsmark

A GODSFIELD BOOK
www.godsfieldpress.com

For my mom, who made sure there was always a dog in
the house, my dad, a man whose presence will always be
missed, and Pepper, Ruby and Barney.

First published in Great Britain in 2004
by Godsfield Press,
a division of Octopus Publishing Group Ltd
2–4 Heron Quays
Docklands
London E14 4JP

2 4 6 8 10 9 7 5 3

Printed and bound in China

ISBN 1 84181 239 0
EAN 9781841812397

Contents

Introduction

I used to walk home from school. There was a shortcut that snaked through the woods, emptying out into the turn-around at the top of our gravelled, dead-end street. My house was to the right, and it had large picture windows in the front. There was always one thing I could count on, no matter what kind of day I'd had at school: my dog, Ruby, would be staring intently out of the window, waiting for me to come home.

She'd watch me emerge from the woods and make my way across the gravel. I could see her black head and red tongue even through the reflection of the trees that painted the surface of the glass. She would time me, making sure there were as few seconds as possible where I was out of sight. She'd bolt for the door just as the doorknob turned.

Then I'd watch her motor go. When she was extremely happy, she didn't just wag her tail, she'd wag her entire back end, as if her poor tail didn't have a prayer of containing all the enthusiasm she felt at my return.

I can't remember a time when I was a kid that we didn't have a dog. They were such a vital part of my family's life, and are intricately woven into my memories of that happy time.

I was quite young when Pepper joined my family. My memories of her aren't as clear as they are of the effervescent Ruby. But her gentleness and her sweet, loving nature stand out clearly. She was the perfect dog for a house full of young kids. She played with enthusiasm, but never nipped a clumsy childish hand. She had a calm, nurturing strength, as if we were her puppies and she our mother. I learned the meaning of a broken heart when she passed away.

After I moved away from home, my Mom got Barney. He was part wolf, born in the mountains of Colorado and transplanted to our home in Wisconsin. Barney was a superb hunter, and had the pack mentality of the wolf firmly in his psyche. Mom was the alpha leader, and he was devoted to her with a single-mindedness I'd never seen before.

I lived far away in California at that point, so I was only able to visit once or twice a year. Yet Barney never greeted me as a stranger. I was part of his pack and, therefore, much celebrating, licking, leaning, jumping and petting would ensue. He was always blissful when we were together.

One of his favourite pastimes was to be brushed, and I would spend long sessions with him. He was such a large dog, but when he was brushed, he would loll on the carpet, legs every which way, quietly tasting nirvana.

He, too, had a gentleness that was belied by his size. Wolves allow the pups in their pack to do anything they please. Barney was incredibly tolerant of my family's new generation, as they passed from fur-grabbing toddlers to enthusiastic playmates. Kids and dogs at play – is there anything more fun to watch?

I began learning from my dogs at a very young age. Pepper, Ruby and Barney were all great teachers, as they showed me the importance of loyalty, enthusiasm, affection, honesty and obedience. They showed me how to be patient and to pursue my dreams. They showed me how to fall instantly in love, and how to deal with my grief when an old friend passes away.

This book is my way of passing on these valuable teachings. Dogs have so many positive and enriching characteristics. If you pay attention to what they are saying, they have a lot of answers to life's questions.

If you're like me, your dog is a very special presence in your life. He is a member of your family, a trusted friend and a source of infinite, selfless love. I hope these lessons from my dogs will help you in your spiritual journey, as they did me. And if you have any questions on the material, just ask your pooch.

Man's best friend

f you're familiar with Greek mythology, you probably know the story of Odysseus (Ulysses). After the Trojan War ended, Odysseus sailed the seas for 20 long years, trying to return to his kingdom on the island of Ithaca. Finally, the odyssey ended and he was ashore.

Arduous suitors, thinking Odysseus was long dead, filled Ithaca, all vying for the hand of Odysseus' wife and queen, Penelope. Odysseus, changed beyond recognition by his travels, disguised himself as a beggar, fooling everyone he met, including his wife and son.

But there was one in the kingdom who recognized him: Argus, Odysseus' aged and dying hound dog. Unable to stand, Argus greeted the return of his master with perked ears and a wag of his old tail. His own journey of waiting completed, Argus died, happy at last.

That's how it is with dogs, isn't it? People will change, relationships fail, children move away, but your dog – well, your dog is loyal to his last breath. Imagine what the world would be like were people as loyal and steadfast as your canine companion. It's quite possible that many of the world's problems would evaporate.

Loyalty, real and imagined

What if every person you met was dependable and constant? What if no one would willingly deceive or betray you? How many of your relationships would change? How many would stay the same?

If your answers are weighted towards the former and not the latter, perhaps it's time for a change. If you surround yourself with disloyal or deceptive people, how can you invest them with the trust necessary for a healthy relationship? Mistrust chips away at your spirit, leaving you forever wary, on edge, and projecting motives on to those around you.

Everyone projects sometimes. You can't help it, because your past and your own experiences colour your reactions to new situations. If, for example, your spouse cheated on you, always giving you an excuse about working late, it's difficult not to worry about a new partner who also claims to be working late. It's easy to begin projecting your ex's behaviour on to this new person, jumping to conclusions without any real information.

Histories are more full of examples of the fidelity of dogs than of friends.

ALEXANDER POPE, POET AND AUTHOR (1688–1744)

There is no faith which has never yet been broken except that
of a truly faithful dog.

KONRAD LORENZ, ZOOLOGIST AND NOBEL LAUREATE (1903–1989)

Challenges come if you spend all your energy projecting, and reacting to the 'reality' you just invented. Do this too often and there will be nothing left in your 'trust fund'. No one likes to appear stupid, and no one wants to be fooled by the same ruse twice. But it is important to see the world as it is, not just through the distorted lens of your own issues.

Trust with awareness

The solution is trust with awareness. There is nothing wrong with being aware of the lessons you've learned in your life, and treating them with respect. But each new situation has to begin with the anticipation of trust. Your dog trusts you to feed him, pet him, play with him and treat him well. In return he gives you his undying devotion, love and protection. His heart and soul are yours. That's his gift to you. Your gift to him is to cherish them.

There are people in your life who have entrusted you with similar gifts. They might be your children, spouse, parents, friends or siblings. Think about who these people specifically are in your life. Have you ever let them down? Lied to them? Said hurtful things to them in anger? If you answer yes to any of these (and who among us cannot?), then consider being a bit more dog-like in your approach.

It's okay to get angry or frustrated when dealing with loved ones. You're human, and human emotions and motives often get little snarls or tangles. But your goal should be to treat the people you love with honour and loyalty. You know from experience that the deepest hurts are inflicted by those closest to you. You have the same power when it comes to those who love you.

Deep inside, Odysseus hadn't changed. He still adored his wife, Penelope, and loved his son dearly. Ithaca, and its people, had always remained close to his heart. But his travels had changed some aspects of the man — enough to make a simple disguise all that was needed to give him the appearance of a stranger. Only his dog, whose heart had remained steadfastly loyal to the true core of the man, was able to see through that disguise.

Don't risk being blind to the people you care about. Don't look at the exterior of your loved ones, as Penelope did, and see only what they are showing on the surface that day. The people in your life are complex, and deserve to be seen with deeper understanding. Look into their hearts in search for the truth. Be steadfast in your support and you will find that dogs have got it right. Loyalty is its own reward.

Exercise: **Tracking your loyalty**

Think about the times in your life when you feel you were disloyal to someone who deserved better from you. Write down the circumstances and why you did what you did. Now try to think of a way that you could have handled the same situation without being disloyal. Try this with all the examples that you thought of. Do you see a theme? Are there any similarities between the events? Do the new solutions feel like better ways to have treated the situation?

In the next few days, try to be conscious of those around you, and of yourself, for examples of disloyalty. Ask yourself if it is real or just your own projection. If you find yourself projecting motives and negative thoughts on others, do your best to consciously subjugate the urge. Try to look at the people in your life through a less-cluttered lens. Learn to trust.

The best things in life are never rationed. Friendship, loyalty and love.
They do not require coupons.

GEORGE T. HEWITT, *THE FORBES BOOK OF BUSINESS QUOTATIONS*

Lesson 2
Obedience school

Sometimes it's easy to forget that a dog is… well, a dog. They're going to bark at inappropriate times. They're going to growl at visitors, or jump up on you with muddy feet, or wolf their food or make a mess on the rug. That's why you train your dog. You teach her to do her business outside, or to stay off the guest's leg, to sit, beg, roll over, and make you a nice dinner. Granted, some tricks work better than others.

You train your dog because you need her to follow your rules. It's the only way you can co-habit with, what would otherwise be, a wild animal. Human society has rules, as well. Laws exist so that the wild animals known as humans don't have to live in anarchy and chaos.

Obeying the law isn't very difficult. Sure, you might break the speed limit, or park where you shouldn't, but you probably weigh the consequences when you do it. If you're speeding, you know that you might get a ticket. It's your choice whether you want to risk that. You also risk having an accident. A sharp turn taken too quickly can be deadly – for you, and for other drivers. That's why there are laws. They're not a conspiracy to curtail your freedom; they're a way to give everyone equal freedom.

The need for rules and laws

Laws protect us from others and ourselves. You wouldn't let your dog rip the throat out of the postman, so there is never a reason for you to get behind the wheel of a car when drunk or high. Both activities can lead to the death of innocents.

A healthy spirit also has a rule, or 'law', it lives by: do no harm. Harming others is a certain way to damage your spirit, sometimes irreparably. But not everything that can do harm is governed by the letters of mankind's laws. There are other rules you must live by, as well.

Lies can harm others, as can cruelty, insults, rudeness and a host of other negative actions. For example, when you go to a restaurant do you treat your server like a human being, or do you order her around, speaking harshly and without feelings? There are many people who take out their frustrations on people in the service industries. If you've ever done this, it's time to examine the reasons behind your actions.

Take a stand

It is not difficult to feel powerless in this world, and that helpless feeling is often the reason why individuals get abusive. Whether it's arguments on the internet, bad-mouthing friends behind their backs or feuding with your neighbours, power displays can often be ugly and fruitless.

This is not to say that there won't be times when you must take a stand. If the cause is just, and you believe in it, you owe it to yourself to make your voice heard. You may have to break some rules to get them changed. You may have to put yourself and your reputation on the line to affect a change. But if you believe in something strongly enough, and you are not doing others harm, it can be a worthwhile task.

History is filled with people who stood up against a greater power and, without violence, changed the world. Gandhi in India and Martin Luther King Jr in the United States are two such examples. Both faced what seemed to be insurmountable odds. Yet both succeeded in ways that their other, more violent, counterparts could never have dreamed.

Your dog has limits to what she will do. She will always be true to herself in the end. When too much is asked of you, you must know who you are and remain true to yourself in the same way. Obey that inner voice that tells you what is right and what is wrong. Follow the rules that make sense, and are for the greater good. But when you run into something you cannot abide, take a stand.

If you see someone else being hurt or abused, do what you can to help. It isn't only you that you must stand up for. Everyone has the capability to make an impact in this world. Whatever your causes, your voice can be heard. You can choose your weapon – whether it's your wallet, your time or just moral support – and you can make an impact.

Exercise: **Do you follow or flaunt the rules?**

Think about some of the choices you've made in your life. Do you tend towards obedience or disobedience? Do you follow every rule regardless of logic or circumstance? Are you a maverick who refuses to comply even if the rules make sense and are there to protect the good of all? Do you fight too much or not enough? Do you expect others to obey but you are the exception?

Think about a time when you deliberately broke a law. Why did you do it? Did you put anyone in harm's way? Were there any consequences? If not, would you have been sorry or defiant if there had been?

Now think of a time when you feel you should have spoken out, but didn't. What made you remain silent? If you had the opportunity to do it again, would you do things differently? Imagine a similar circumstance, but this time any consequences you may have feared would come true. Would you still feel you should speak out or would the consequences keep you silent?

Don't judge yourself when answering these questions. Everyone has a different limit of tolerance towards these difficult situations. What's far more important is that you get a sense of who you are, where you stand and what might affect you in the future. This exercise isn't about being right or wrong, or good or bad. It's about self-knowledge.

The ultimate measure of a man is not where he stands
in moments of comfort and convenience,
but where he stands at times of challenge and controversy.

DR MARTIN LUTHER KING JR, CIVIL RIGHTS LEADER (1929–1968)

Say no to sheep's clothing

There is a wonderful simplicity about how dogs deal with people. If a dog likes you, he wags his tail, licks your hand or jumps for joy. It's easy to think your dog is smiling at you, with his upturned mouth, lolling tongue and sparkling eyes.

If a dog doesn't like you, or mistrusts you, you get growls and barks and bared teeth. There's no way on Earth to misinterpret that message! Sharp canine teeth and delicate human flesh are not a good combination. Wouldn't it be great if people were this open? But they aren't.

Wearing masks

Humans live in a duplicitous world, and often have to wear masks to survive. You wear one mask at work, another with strangers, still another at home – until the picture of who you truly are becomes foggy. In some cases, you don't have a choice. It would be inappropriate to treat the CEO of a company the same way as you treat a five-year-old. You don't want to wear the same expression at a sporting event as you wear at a funeral. So who is the real you when you are just yourself, without any masks? Or are you ever truly bare to the eyes of others?

You might show yourself when you are with your dog. It's easy to let go when you look into that beloved face, isn't it? You might even get the feeling that he sees through any artifice, so it would be a waste of time to wear any mask around him.

There might be people with whom you share this same intimacy. Perhaps it's your spouse, children or a very close friend. Everyone needs someone with whom they can be open and share their secrets. Who is that person in your life? Is it just one person, or do you share parts of yourself with two or three people, and it all adds up to the whole?

The mask of the liar

One of the most harmful masks people wear is that of the liar. Sometimes, you might think a lie is kinder than the truth. They're called 'little white lies' and they can be acceptable under some circumstances. You certainly don't want to hurt someone else's feelings unnecessarily. 'Yes, that dress

We are what we pretend to be, so we must be careful about

what we pretend to be.

KURT VONNEGUT, AUTHOR (B. 1922)

looks nice on you,' you might say to an insecure friend. 'Have you lost weight?' There are plenty of social lies that don't do any measurable harm, and may in fact avoid hurt and pain.

Or do they? Perhaps the person in the dress really wanted to know if it suited her. She might have been looking for an honest appraisal, and not insincere flattery. If you spend too much time telling white lies, your credibility will diminish.

Tell too many white lies and the bigger lies also begin to get easier. You don't want to admit that you overslept, so you say, 'Sorry I was late, but traffic was terrible!' But the bigger the lie, the easier you can get caught. Someone else may have already mentioned that traffic had been light. At that point, being late isn't as important as the fact that you were lying. 'What else have you lied about?' your boss might wonder.

Dishonesty is a trap that can feed on itself. One lie often leads to another and pretty soon you have to keep an entire fictional world intact. I had a friend who lied more easily than she told the truth. She told so many lies that it was impossible to trust anything she said. Yet no matter how obvious the lies; no matter if I confronted her with irrefutable proof; she would swear by her untruths without wavering.

It's difficult to live with that degree of duplicity. There comes a time when the lies are too numerous, and you have to excise that person from your life. Yet a healthy dose of honesty can be enough to overcome many faults. If you're like most people, you like to keep the honest ones around.

Your spirit cannot lie. It is truth incarnate. Lies obscure the purity of your spirit, hiding it behind clouds and fog until, some day, you may wonder what you did to tarnish it so. Don't let that happen. Take a page from your dog's book. Remove your mask when you need to express your affection. Be as honest as you can with those you love. And if a good growl at a stranger would help you steer clear of trouble, then 'grrr' to your heart's content.

Exercise: Talk among yourself

Be open – with yourself as well as with others. Think of all the masks you wear, and the different behaviours you present behind each one. Perhaps you have a Work You, a Home You, a Spouse You, a Parent You, a Sibling You, a Daughter or Son You and a Dog Owner You – there can be any number of them. Pick the most prevalent ones in your life at this time. Write a dialogue between these personas. Don't worry about being clever or a master playwright. Focus instead on capturing the voices and

ideologies. For example, you probably speak differently when talking to your dog than when talking to your boss (I hope so!). Try to capture those different patterns of speech.

When you've got a good conversation going, add the 'real you' – the person you think you really are, underneath everything. Does this real you like these other 'people'? And if you can't answer yes to every one of them, then why do you don that particular mask? What's different about your true voice in relation to the others?

Now ask yourself if any of the other personas is at heart a liar. If so, what caused this? Think about what would happen if you changed this behaviour. Would honesty be welcomed? Or do you have fears that are being covered by the lies? Dig deep on this one, because it is important for the health of yourself and your relationships.

I never let sleeping dogs lie. I always demand they tell me the truth.

ANONYMOUS

33

Lesson 4

Wag your tail

Dogs are very clear communicators. Because they are social animals that evolved with a pack mentality, they 'talk' to each other as a survival mechanism. This is very handy for humans. It is most likely that you appreciate it when you get clear signals from your pet telling you he wants to eat, be petted or go for a walk.

Communication between humans is far more complex. We don't have tails that we can wag, but our faces are capable of hundreds of expressions – all of which can be read, both consciously and subconsciously, by others. Anthropologists postulate that human society gained a great deal of complexity when the whites around our eyes grew. This allowed the 'windows to the soul' a far greater range of expression and emotion.

Things really took off when we developed speech and language. What surely began as rudimentary vocabulary aided by non-verbal signals has grown into something so complex, it's a wonder we understand as much as we do. For example, the unabridged *Oxford English Dictionary* has about 600,000 words — and that's just English. Add the rest of the world's languages and it's easy to understand why good communication can be so tricky.

Yet clear communication is extremely important in our human society. Nothing can mess things up more quickly or explosively than poor communication. From flame wars on the internet, to marital discord and a business deal turned sour — poor communication is often at the root of many problems. Too bad we don't have tails.

Communication and trust

One thing that can get in the way of clear communication is trust. If you don't trust what you are saying, it will be difficult to get others to believe you. Self-doubt can creep into the messages you send, creating mistrust from your listener. By the same token, if you don't trust the message you are receiving, there will also be unclear communication.

These trust issues can arise at all the levels of communication. You may doubt the information you are hearing, and question the relationship you have with the speaker.

One reason the dog has so many friends:

he wags his tail instead of his tongue.

ANONYMOUS

Your dog won't wag her tail for false reasons. There may be times when you don't quite understand what she wants, but generally this is due to your missing some subtle signs, and is not your dog's fault.

With humans, a person can say one thing and mean something completely different. Imagine you're at a party, and you are about to tell a story. 'Do you want to hear this?' you ask. 'Oh, yes, please,' is the answer. But even as the words are spoken, you notice the person's eyes searching the room, his body is turned partially away from you and his voice is empty of enthusiasm. His words said, 'Yes,' but everything else is telling you, 'No.' Therefore, you don't trust his words.

In another scenario, you are on an internet message board and someone says something nasty to you. You take umbrage with the insult. He responds, 'I was just joking.' Had this exchange happened in person, you might have seen a twinkle in his eye and a smile on his lips. His voice may have had good-natured warmth. Just a little harmless sarcasm, his body is telling you.

In online interactions, you don't have these extra clues. If you are well acquainted, and have a good history, you probably won't misinterpret the comments. But without that, and without the non-verbal signposts, the mutual communication breaks down completely.

Working towards better communication

So what can you do? Make sure that your goal is always to have successful communication, not just 'I want my say!' You need to be aware of the other person, whether he is the listener or the speaker, and you need to trust both yourself and him. If you can't trust yourself, don't say it. And if you can't trust him, then ask yourself why that person might be lying.

If the communication is written, as is online interaction, be especially careful what you write. Without the visual clues available in person, it's easy to be misunderstood. No one can see your smile or the sparkle in your eyes. That means your words alone have to convey your message and its meaning. Always read your message before hitting 'send', to make sure it will be understood. Use proper grammar and spelling, avoid sarcasm (sarcasm is extremely dependent on external clues, such as voice and facial expressions), and do your best not to write when angry.

If you communicate clearly, it will strengthen many aspects of your life. Miscommunication can destroy relationships, breed negative emotions and can pull you into a quagmire of misunderstanding. By saying what you mean, and meaning what you say, you will find that most people will respond to you with trust and respect.

Exercise: **A practice letter**

Imagine that a friend just told you that your dog knocked over her rubbish bins. She didn't get a good look at the dog, but it was the same colour and size as yours, so she assumed it was your dog. Your job is to write her a letter, explaining why your dog is innocent. Use your imagination to fill in the details, but concentrate on being as clear and concise as you can, without resorting to anger or negative emotions. Remember, you want to trust what you say, so don't exaggerate or offer false proofs. Be sympathetic to her problem, but make sure there will be no opportunity for her to misunderstand your position.

For the next week, put this into practice and try to make all your communication – verbal, non-verbal and written – as clear as you can. Did it help make the week smoother? If so, in what way? Now read over the letter you wrote in this exercise. Is there anything you would change? Did you keep your anger out of it? Has a week of clearer communication given you a better understanding of how to write a letter like that?

Lesson 5
Go fetch!

Dogs love to play. They like to run, jump, catch things, and triumphantly return them to you for another round. They will play until exhausted, yet still probably wish they could do it all again. Play is as vital to a dog's health as food, water and sleep. It's how their wild counterparts learned to hunt and socialize in the pack. Their instincts tell them to hone their skills, and their love for you makes shared games pure joy. In short, dogs know how to have fun.

You may know how to have fun, too, but do you allow yourself enough of it? It's important to play, and to let go of your everyday worries. You can define your fun by whatever parameters you prefer. Some people like to play sports, others to watch them. Some like to do puzzles or play video games. Others like to swim, hike or fly a plane. It doesn't matter how you define your personal game of fetch, just make sure that you allow it into your life. Joy and exuberance are far too valuable to be possessed by dogs alone.

Why you need to play

It's so easy to get caught up in a workaholic haze. Your work is one of the ways in which you define yourself. People use their jobs as self-descriptions: 'I'm a sales executive', '…a mother' or '…a lawyer'. You don't say, 'I work as a lawyer', you say 'I *am* a lawyer' as if that's all that you are.

Stay-at-home parents can be even more trapped in their jobs because they rarely get away. There's no separate place to go to do your work. From morning to night, you are a mother, doing a mother's work, and by the time the kids are asleep you barely have the energy to do anything else.

That's why playing is so important. It allows you to let go of your ordinary life for a space of time, so that you can concentrate on something a bit more inconsequential. If you're a business executive who likes to play golf on the weekends, then you know that that time isn't filled with paperwork and meetings – it's about your swing, fresh air, camaraderie, and a hundred other things that have nothing to do with the daily grind.

Or maybe you're a mother who steals 20 minutes to soak in a hot bath, reading a good novel or doing a crossword puzzle. The tension escapes into the enervating heat, your mind gets wrapped up in the words on the page and, finally, you can let go of the constant stream of demands.

The greatest pleasure of a dog is that you may make a fool of

yourself with him, and not only will he not scold you,

but he will make a fool of himself, too.

SAMUEL BUTLER, AUTHOR (1835–1902)

47

Perhaps you're one of those people who can't let go. If you're not worried about something, you worry about the fact that you're not worrying. It's impossible to relax, because relaxing won't solve your problems. My question is, does worrying solve them? If you're worried about not having enough money, does that state of mind automatically generate more funds? Of course it doesn't. It just means that you're unhappy all the time.

Essential play

It is essential for the health of your spirit to feed it joy and relaxation. Play a sport, letting the game be your only concern, and you'll not only exercise your body, but you'll give your mind a much-needed rest. Read a good piece of fiction, play a game or do a puzzle, and you'll exercise your mind while giving your hard-working body the night off. You know what you need when it comes to relaxation. Don't just think about it, do it.

Watch your dog when you play with her. She's energized and focused on the moment. The stick you just threw isn't the goal; it's all about being with you. She knows that when the two of you play, she is your focus. She gets to chase and jump and run and she is in dog heaven. That's a perfect way to play.

Let the play take over your thoughts and actions while you're in the midst of it and you'll be able to let go of pressure and tension. When you truly embrace your ability to play, you'll be able to switch off your worries by singing a song or laughing with a friend.

One of the marvellous benefits of play is that it allows your subconscious to work on some of those daily problems. It's a wonderful feeling to be in the middle of a game of fetch and realize that you've just thought of a solution to a work snarl, or decided what ingredient is missing from that recipe you were wanting to cook. Sometimes your conscious mind keeps your subconscious silent, so the only way to access this deeper, spiritual force is to take your conscious mind 'off line'. Play is an excellent way to do this.

Make sure you engage in both physical and mental play, so that you have a good balance. Both will keep you healthier as you age, will allow your subconscious to work for you and will strengthen your spirit.

Work consists of whatever a body is obliged to do.
Play consists of whatever a body is not obliged to do.
MARK TWAIN, HUMORIST AND AUTHOR (1835–1910)

Exercise: **It's time to play!**

Include at least one physical and one mental game in your schedule in the following week. Record your feelings after playing. Was it exhilarating? Did you feel better? Less stressed? Did you feel a sense of accomplishment? If your reactions were positive, then consider adding more activities like these to your schedule.

If your reactions were negative, ask yourself why you were unable to enjoy playing. Did you feel guilty? Do you fear that a little play will lead to more until you'll get no work done at all? Once you have thought about why you were unable to enjoy a bit of playing, think about an activity that you have enjoyed in the past. Why were you able to play then, but not now? What circumstances have changed? Or was it simply that one activity is okay, and another is not?

Now try an activity that you have enjoyed in the past, making sure the circumstances are comfortable (such as getting a babysitter you trust, or making sure there's no pressing work left on your desk) and try again. Relax, let go and have fun.

Lesson 6
Puppy love

f there is one thing at which dogs excel, it's showing unconditional love and affection. And the chances are, you're pretty good at showing the same to them. So why can it be difficult to be that open and loving with other humans? Your dog asks for affection and gets it instantly, yet it's easy to be too busy, too conflicted or too distracted to give spouses, children, parents or friends this same attention. Why is there such a vast difference between pets and people in such a basic area?

The answer to this conundrum is rooted in the relationship you share with your pet versus the people in your life. With your dog, things are rather simple. A pat on the head or a scratch behind the ears is often enough. And he doesn't ask for your undivided attention. You can pet your dog and carry on a conversation with someone without losing any of your focus. When you have time to put your dog centre stage, as when you feed him or play with him, he'll be there.

The barriers

With people, things are much more complicated. You might have barriers to unfettered affection that stand in your way. Perhaps you are shy, repressed, too proud, too distracted, and so on. Sometimes you might feel like you always give and never receive. Sometimes you're too tired from a busy day and feel that having to express your love can be a burden. Whatever the reason, it stands in the way of the easy affection you might otherwise express.

There are social barriers as well. Petting your dog in public is to be expected. But doing some heavy petting with your significant other can be an intrusive public display to bystanders. Or perhaps you're not comfortable showing too much affection in front of your children. There are many reasons for holding back, and some are quite valid. The trick is to make sure you don't withhold so much that you find yourself in a world without touch or words of affection. You need it as much as your dog does. It is essential you find a balance between your needs and your sensibilities.

One of the biggest barriers to showing love is the fear of being hurt. The closer you are to someone, the easier and more frequent the opportunities to get hurt. But protecting yourself from hurt by eschewing love is far more painful in the long run. Instead of focusing on how you can be hurt, focus instead on filling your life with people who will love you without causing excessive pain.

Affection held hostage

When you hear a battered woman interviewed, you often hear her say, 'But I love him. And he always feels so sorry afterwards, I just had to forgive him.' Most abusers don't stop their behaviour, yet the battered woman believes his promises. These promises are often sincere at the time they are said but are almost always forgotten the next time the abuser feels powerless. With such a weakened spirit, he can only find power in domination over another soul.

Kindness, respect, honour and the ability to love strengthen the spirit. If you have this inner strength, you will find it easier to show affection to those who deserve it. And you will have the courage to choose people who have enough personal strength that they don't need to 'borrow' yours. There are people in this world who beat their dogs. You wouldn't stand for that, would you? So don't ever let anyone beat you, whether physically, emotionally, mentally or spiritually.

Your task is not to seek for love, but merely to seek and find
all of the barriers within yourself that you have built against it.

JALAL UD-DIN RUMI, POET (1207–1273)

By the same token, withholding love can also be a type of power struggle. The famous Greek play, *Lysistrata*, told the story of a group of women who tired of their husbands going off to war. The women decided to abstain from sex until their husbands battled no more. The play is a comedy but the message of 'affection held hostage' is a powerful one. Love and affection are necessary for everyone – male and female, young and old, healthy and ill. Everyone needs to feel the touch of another human, hear some kind words and see an affectionate gaze.

Self-love

There is one more form of love that is essential, and that is self-love. If your inner voice feeds you a steady stream of put-downs and negative thoughts, it becomes very difficult for you to show love to others. It's imperative to turn those thoughts around. For every negative you can think of, there is a positive that could be taking its place. It may take some hard work, but if you consciously choose to stop your negative self-talk, you could change your entire outlook on life.

With a positive change towards self-love, you will find that loving others is no longer very difficult. You'll want to give attention to your family and friends because your heart will be free instead of weighed down by negatives. Every relationship in your life could be uplifted with this one simple change.

Exercise: **Show your puppy love**

It's time to show some puppy love for the people in your life who deserve your affection. Do something special for each person, tailored to fit his or her wishes and desires (be sure this is about them, and not just you).

A friend might enjoy a nice dinner, with a long, chatty conversation. Your spouse might appreciate a love letter, filled with honest emotion. Your child might revel in a one-on-one play session, or a trip to the zoo or museum. Your parent might delight in an evening of home movies or slides, filled with precious memories. It's up to you to work out what is needed and how you can show each person how special he or she is to you.

Finally, show yourself the same love you just showed others. Do something you've been wanting to do for ages but never found the time. Indulge yourself as a token of your own self-love.

If you aren't good at loving yourself, you will have a difficult time loving

anyone, since you'll resent the time and energy you give another person

that you aren't even giving to yourself.

BARBARA DE ANGELIS PHD, RELATIONSHIP EXPERT AND AUTHOR

Lesson 7
Hot diggity dog

s there any creature more capable of showing happiness than a dog? She can be transported to Heaven with just a moment of consideration from her owner. Play with her, pet her or brush her, and she is the happiest creature on Earth. Consider your own dog and the messages she gives you. How many of those messages are pure, unadulterated joy? Do you show your joy this often, and with such clarity? If not, why not?

In our society, showing joy and enthusiasm is frowned upon by many people. You're looked at as strange, odd or mentally unbalanced if you show too much. Walk down the street singing, and see what sort of looks you get – probably a lot of rolling eyes, disapproving frowns or giggles.

Well, there's no sense being looked at as a nut! So how can you show your enthusiasm and still be considered sane? Chances are, you are so used to damping down strong emotions that it wouldn't be difficult to 'up' your joy levels and still appear quite functional.

Demonstrative joy

Watch the players on a game show when they win. Each player reacts differently. Some will leap out of their chairs or bound around the studio with enthusiasm so enormous it can barely be contained within the human body.

Other winners will just smile a lot. No bouncing, leaping or gigantic reaction, yet they are probably equally as joyful. Which contestant is more fun to watch? Which would you rather work with, see at a party or play a sport with?

It's going to depend on your personality as to which is your answer. But consider this: joy and enthusiasm are contagious. It's nearly impossible not to feel some of that radiated happiness when you are near someone who is experiencing such a strong emotion. And when you feel this powerful force pouring towards you, seeping into you – you, too, will feel joyous. Your energy rises, your smile widens and laughter and a sense of well-being follow.

It's such a wonderful feeling, too! It's like being greeted by a dog with a wildly wagging tail. It's nearly impossible not to feel some of the energy from your dog seeping into you. You give a good rough pet and a pat, put

Joy is not in things; it is in us.

RICHARD WAGNER, COMPOSER (1813–1883)

your voice in that 'I'm talking to my dog to get her excited' tone, and the two of you feed off each other. That's what enthusiasm is, and that's the feeling that you should embrace it.

Simple joy

Many people think that joy should be reserved for big events. 'If I get a promotion, then I'll be happy!' Or 'Just wait until the baby is born – I won't be able to contain myself!'. That's to be expected, and of course you should show immense joy at big events. But what about all those millions of small moments that get passed by while you're waiting for something big to happen? Do you ever give them their due?

Acknowledging simple joys can make the difference between a person who is just existing and one who is living life to the fullest. Think about your dog again and ask yourself if he is waiting for some enormous event – or is he just waiting for you to get home? Do you think his joy would be any less because you were only gone for a few hours? Your dog probably considers your homecoming a major highlight! With all that wagging and happiness flowing out of him – how can you doubt it? Just the sight of you is enough to rock his world!

Curb your dog, not your enthusiasm

You can feel as happy as your hound. You can take every simple joy and greet it with enthusiasm. Have you ever eaten a really good sandwich, watched a funny TV show, had fun playing a board game, looked at your child while she's sleeping or tilted your face to the summer sun? None of these are life-changing events, but all are infinite sources of simple joy.

The trick is not to let them flow past you without consciously feeling the happiness. It's human nature to dwell too deeply on the negatives. But instead of thinking about everything that went wrong, or wasn't as good as you expected, start thinking about the things that went right.

Every day is filled with successes and failures. By concentrating only on the failures, it becomes difficult to celebrate the successes. And you need those celebrations to retain the energy to keep chasing the bigger joys.

Exulting in simple joys and living with enthusiasm are two things your dog does instinctively. You can, too. It might take a little conscious thought at first, but eventually it'll become so easy that it'll be second nature. Every success will be celebrated. Every task will be undertaken with zeal. Every relationship will be nurtured with passion. And suddenly there will be nothing ordinary about your life.

Nothing great was ever achieved without enthusiasm.

RALPH WALDO EMERSON, AUTHOR, POET AND PHILOSOPHER (1803–1882)

Exercise: **Celebrating the ordinary**

List ten good things that have happened to you in the past three days. They don't have to be big. They can be downright inconsequential. The items on this list are things that made you happy, even if momentarily. For example, you realized that the cantaloupe you bought was at the absolute right stage of ripeness. Your car mileometer just flipped to a number that had all zeros behind it. Your toddler just said something funny. Or a line on television made you laugh out loud.

Study your list of ten 'ordinary' good things. Did you celebrate any of the items with enthusiasm? If not, why? If you can master the art of experiencing simple joy and enthusiasm, your life has the potential of being filled with 'good things' instead of overflowing with negatives.

In the next week, be aware of things that make you happy and your reactions to them. If necessary, try to make a puppy-like adjustment. Think of the daily greeting your dog gives you, and use it as a guide to help discover your own capacity for simple joy and enthusiasm.

Lesson 8
Work like a dog

Dogs aren't just pets. Some dogs are used by law enforcement to sniff out drugs or capture suspects. Some are seeing-eye dogs, helping the blind weave their way through a sighted world. Some are cadaver dogs, finding victims of crime or disaster. Some help the disabled, perform in circuses, are athletes, make rescues, and some are even used to help diagnose illnesses. Each of these dogs does something to help humankind.

Imagine what the world would be like if people were as selfless as dogs? Happily, you can be. You have talents and skills that not everyone possesses. You have a job – whether it's in an office, raising children, going to school or even just looking for your niche. You might do regular service for your community, or you may place your concentration on your own family's needs. Whatever you want out of life, work as hard as these special dogs and the world will be better because you lived.

Do your best work

If you don't have a service-oriented job, don't worry. It isn't about what your job is, but how you do it and how you live your life. It's about your talents, skills and your desire to make the world just a little bit better.

There are some very special dogs that illustrate this perfectly. After the terrorist attacks in New York City on September 11, 2001, rescue dogs looked for survivors in the rubble of the World Trade Towers. They worked tirelessly, crawling over unstable piles of smouldering steel and concrete, sniffing for any signs of life. Unfortunately, the devastation was so complete, there were very few survivors.

The dogs became depressed about not finding any live bodies. To keep them engaged in their task, their handlers would 'bury' themselves. Triumphant barks would ring out and a 'live victim' would emerge from the rubble. It's a measure of how hard these dogs worked, and how much they cared about their 'jobs'. Nothing else mattered to them – not the dust-clogged air or their bleeding paws. They lived to rescue.

Think about your own jobs (not just where you work, but your job as part of a family, a community, and humankind). Do you work hard even if you're tired, unhappy, bored or angry? If you're a parent, do you always

Attempt the impossible in order to improve your work.

BETTE DAVIS, ACTRESS (1908–1989)

do your best to raise children who will be an asset to the world? Do you treat everyone around you with honesty and respect? Do you have the same kind of dogged enthusiasm as the canine rescue squad?

If you're like most people, you've probably been a victim of someone who didn't live his life this way. Maybe a thief stole your car radio, you got ripped off on an internet auction site or got into a fight over something that wasn't your fault. Everyone is a victim at some point, and it feels lousy, doesn't it? Remember that feeling and do your utmost never to inflict it on another. Don't make it an 'I deserved that' moment. Don't deserve it. Take a lesson from those marvellous, helpful dogs and do whatever you can to serve humankind.

Self-sabotage

It's difficult to find the energy to attack every job with enthusiasm. Sometimes, you might consider failing so that you aren't asked to do it again. Or perhaps it feels too difficult, overwhelming, or you simply don't have the self-esteem necessary to believe that you will succeed.

Self-sabotage is an insidious challenge that must be overcome. If you fall prey to this, you probably berate yourself for being a failure, lazy or not up to the task. In reality, it is more likely fear that is at the heart of the problem. Success can bring changes to your life. It can feel unfamiliar, frightening and can affect your relationships. Fear can start in childhood from parents who weren't supportive or didn't believe in you. There are many sources of fear, but its effects are almost always detrimental to your success.

It's easier not to work hard enough, miss deadlines or avoid your responsibilities. Yet in the end, you are left with an empty feeling. You feel angry, disappointed and worthless — all because of the fears that hide deep within you.

Hard work is its own reward

If you don't suffer from self-sabotage, there are other things that can stand in your way. You might be someone who thinks only of the rewards, and never of the journey. If those rewards don't materialize, you might feel cheated and angry. 'Why should I even try?'

If you don't try, you will never succeed. And if you don't give every project your all, you will never know the satisfaction of working to the limits of your abilities. It's a very special feeling to know that you gave something your very best effort.

The rescue dogs may not have found many live victims, but every time they found a body, a family was gratefully able to bury a loved one. They got closure, and were able to mourn. It was the most important thing in the world to those families. And they had some very hard-working dogs to thank for it.

Exercise: **Working towards goals**

Write down your life goals. Next, write down intermediate goals that will help you achieve those life goals. Finally, write your immediate goals – things you can accomplish in the next week or two. Look at the three lists and ask yourself if these goals are being served by your present lifestyle. If not, what adjustments can you make to help you achieve them?

In the following week, check off each of the short-term goals that you accomplish. Then add a new goal in its place. In Lesson 9, you'll learn more about working towards the goals on the other two lists. Eventually, you want to be able to integrate the three lists, so that each goal serves another.

Teaching old dogs new tricks

I t can be a challenge changing the habits of a dog. Once they learn something, it gets stuck in their brains, unwilling to be dislodged. They have schedules, behaviours and habits that define their day. This can be very helpful. A house-trained dog is a beautiful thing. But other habits are less appreciated by frustrated owners.

Despite this predisposition towards learned habits, dogs are not as stodgy as some people think. Given the right reward, most dogs will do what it takes to earn it. If this means learning a new trick, or modifying a behaviour, then the dog will do what's needed.

People can get trapped in habits and behaviours, too. As with dogs, some of them are good, while others are detrimental. However, you have a distinct advantage over your canine partner. Human beings are the most adaptable species on Earth. We live on every continent, in every extreme from bitter cold to boiling heat. We can be found in massive cities or in complete isolation. We've climbed the highest peaks and explored the bottom of the ocean.

Human beings are engineered for change. If you don't like something about yourself or your life, you have the capacity and freedom to change it. If there's something you've always wanted, you have the ability to pursue it. If there are obstacles in your way, you can overcome them. You can do whatever it takes to learn new tricks.

Goals

When you teach your dog a trick or a desired behaviour, you begin with a goal. Whatever you do to get there, you have to first decide on what you want your dog to accomplish. It's the same with your own life. Without setting clear goals, you'll most likely find yourself drifting from task to task in aimless patterns. It's an unsatisfying way to live, as it lacks structure, purpose and mindfulness.

For the exercise in Lesson 8, you wrote down your goals. Were they all reasonable, or did you think, 'I'll never be able to accomplish all that!' Many people set goals that are too high. By setting impossible goals it

alleviates the need to accomplish them. Rather than work hard and fail, you get to lament and complain about failure without lifting a finger. Don't let this be you.

You've already set goals and achieved them, because you've trained your dog. It may have taken a while with some of the trickier behaviours, but you stuck to it and you got to the finish line. It's time to turn that same goal-oriented philosophy on yourself.

Change

One of the things that might be standing in the way of achieving your goals is fear of change. Change can be frightening. What happens if the goal changes your relationships, time management or location — there's no telling what could happen. If these are your fears, ask yourself if the goal is worth it. If it is, then don't fear the changes it might bring. After all, change doesn't have to be bad. It can be quite wonderful!

A life without change can be a stagnant one. And even that isn't quite true, as change is a never-ending constant in every life. Each day that passes you are a day older. You have memories that weren't there the day before, might have picked up a little knowledge from that documentary you watched on television, or advanced your career with that paper you wrote at work. Small changes are still changes.

Instead of fearing change, embrace it. For example, what if you'd always had a hankering to learn a foreign language? Instead of fearing that you wouldn't be able to do it or dreading the amount of time and effort it would take, think of the positive effects instead. You could speak to people you couldn't have spoken to before. You could travel, read literature in that language – you might even get a job translating! The possibilities are yours to explore.

It's time to decide to be the old dog that has no fear of new tricks. Start setting goals that will improve your life. Embrace whatever changes they bring. And welcome learning into your heart. Your goals can be small or large, but make sure they are achievable. Don't give yourself an excuse for failure before you begin. Once you achieve one goal, you can always set another. The sky may be the limit, but it still takes several steps to reach the sky.

While you're at it, maybe you can teach your dog a new trick or two. She'd probably love the attention. You know she'd like the rewards. And perhaps both of you might learn a few things in the process.

Exercise: Learn something new

Think of something you've always wanted to learn. Perhaps it's another language, or you've always wanted to know how to knit. Maybe you'd like to know how to change a car tyre. Or you could find a work-related goal you'd love to achieve. It can be anything. 'I'll get to it some day.' Well, that day could be now, if you'll let it. It doesn't have to be grandiose. It can be as simple as learning a new recipe, or as grand as learning how to do brain surgery. It doesn't matter, as long as you have the desire and the means to make it happen.

Feel free to begin with baby steps. For example, if you wanted to learn a language, start by memorizing a few words or phrases. When you're comfortable with that, learn a few more. When you're ready to take a bigger step, buy a computer program that teaches it, or enroll in a class. Fit it into your schedule, but fulfil that desire. Life is too short to pack everything you want into uncertain tomorrows.

To accomplish great things, we must not only act, but also dream;
not only plan, but also believe.

ANATOLE FRANCE, FRENCH WRITER, CRITIC AND NOBEL LAUREATE (1844–1924)

Lesson 10
A dog's life

There are few phrases as objectionable as 'just a dog' when it comes to dealing with the loss of your pet. They are never 'just' dogs. They are friends, companions, children and any number of other titles. They have one paw planted firmly in our hearts from the moment they enter our lives.

To me, the most difficult aspect of owning a pet is dealing with loss. When your dog dies, something inside you dies with it. Each animal leaves you with memories that will never be erased. And you have an overwhelming need to keep on making memories with that beloved soul. How do you get through this pain?

Dealing with grief and loss is a universal aspect of the human condition. Most of us suffer through the various stages, hoping to find peace eventually. It takes time, distance and a willingness to love again; but it can be survived.

Many people think that the way to deal with the loss of a pet is to immediately replace him with another. Psychologists caution against this approach. It is important for you to go through the grief process before finding another dog, so that you can deal with the loss in a healthy manner. A new dog will never be exactly like the one that died. It cannot replace your old friend. But it can become a new friend – and you want to be there for that new friend instead of trying to transform him into something he is not.

The five stages of grief

The first stage is denial. It is very difficult to accept that this warm presence that is so much a part of your life won't be there any more. So you might keep his dish full of food, jingle his lead, or start at any sounds, thinking it's him. This is a natural reaction to loss, and shouldn't be a source of shame or thoughts of 'I'm going crazy!' You aren't. You simply don't want him to be gone.

The second stage is anger. You might look for someone to blame, such as your vet, your spouse, your kids or even yourself. You desperately want it to be someone's fault, so that you can target all those negative feelings.

If your anger is turned inwards, it can be very unhealthy. It's better to let those feelings out, rather than hold them inside to fester.

The third stage is bargaining. If you believe in a deity, then it's usually a bargain with God. You offer whatever you have just to hear that bark again or feel that slobbery tongue on your hand. It doesn't matter that the bargain can never be made – you want it so badly you're willing to promise anything, just on the off chance.

The fourth stage is the most difficult: depression. You feel tired and separated from everything around you, as if you're living in a deep, dark tunnel. You may burst into tears at the smallest things, especially if something reminds you of the dog that is no longer there. Most likely, she was a source of great comfort to you in her life, so there is the unbalanced feeling of wanting your dog to help you through the loss of your dog. You might start blaming yourself for her death, thinking you should have done something more to save her.

The final stage is acceptance. This is when you realize that she is gone, and nothing will bring her back. You know that you must press on. The depression lifts and you find yourself able to enjoy things again, laughing again and feeling 'human' again. Acceptance doesn't mean you loved your dog any less. It is the only healthy outcome to the grief process. After all, your dog didn't want you to spend your life in despair while she lived. Why would she want that after her death?

This is when you can begin considering finding a new dog. As a dog-owner, you know that their life spans are far shorter than yours. You know that you will have to deal with loss. But you also know the incalculable harvest of joy a dog will give you in his lifetime. You know that it's worth it.

Your dog as therapist

Dogs are a great help when you are grieving over something else. Your dog is there for you to hug and hold when you feel empty inside. I have a friend who was going through a divorce and she cited her dog as the most important factor towards healing her pain. Her husband may have left her, but her dog stood by her steadfastly, as loving as always.

Some say that dogs have a sixth sense about the emotional needs of their masters. Have you ever been sad or depressed and suddenly your dog was there, leaning against you, comforting you with his eyes and nuzzling muzzle? If your spirit needs healing and comfort, your dog will be there for you. He is, after all, so much more than 'just a dog'. He is your best friend.

There is no psychiatrist in the world like a puppy licking your face.

BERN WILLIAMS, PHILOSOPHER (B. 1929)

Exercise: **A tribute**

Write an essay about any dog you've ever owned. Write about that first day, when you made the decision to take that particular animal into your life. What made him special? What was her funniest moment? What did he like to eat? Where was her favourite spot to sleep? There are no rules as to what you can write about. Just make your dog live on the page. If this dog has passed, you'll have a wonderful tribute to a dear friend. If this is your current pet, you might find comfort in these words some time down the road. Just keep in mind that this isn't an exercise about death. It is a celebration of your dog's life.

The pain passes, but the beauty remains.

PIERRE AUGUSTE RENOIR, IMPRESSIONIST PAINTER (1841–1919)

Index

Acknowledgements

Every reasonable effort has been made to acknowledge the ownership of copyright material included in this book. Any errors that have inadvertently occurred will be corrected in subsequent editions provided notification is sent to the publisher.

Goodman, Edward C. (Editor), *The Forbes Book of Business Quotations: 14,173 Thoughts on the Business of Life*, Black Dog & Leventhal Pub; 1997
King, Martin Luther, Jr., *Autobiography of Martin Luther King, Jr.*, Warner Books; 1998
Vonnegut, Kurt, *Mother Night*, Harper & Row, 1966
Twain, Mark, *The Adventures of Tom Sawyer*, American Publishing Company, 1876

Picture acknowledgements

Alamy/Andrew Catterall 32
Corbis UK Ltd/Bettman 60, Cordaiy Photo Library/Paul Kaye 10, /Tim Davis 82, /John Drysdale 81, /Charles Mann 41, /Bill Miles 1, 63, /Kevin Muggleton 2, 13, /Terry Vine front cover
Getty Images 9, 14, 47, 67, /Robert Daly 56, /K Dan-Bergman 64, /Evans 70, /Frank Herholdt 68, /Morgan Mazzoni 86, /Joe McBride 48/, Bryan Mullennix 24, /Sean Murphy 78, /Tamara Reynolds 52, /VCL/Chris Tubbs 18, /Ian Tyas 91, /Simon Watson 38, /Chaloner Woods 23
Magnum Photos/Elliott Erwitt 34, 92
Photonica/Henry Horenstein 26, 37, /McGregor & Gordon 5
Retna UK/National Magazines/Country Living/Charlie Colmer 42
Rex Features/Richard Austin 44, /Mike Daines 29, /Verity Reily 73, /White and Red 59
TopFoto/Eastcott-Momatiuk/The Image Works 76

Executive Editor Brenda Rosen
Managing Editor Clare Churly
Executive Art Editor Sally Bond
Designer Pia Hietarinta for Cobalt id
Senior Production Controller Ian Paton